VAULTING THE TREADMILL

Grace Westerduin's responses to vistas and voices all over the place are contained here, in what feels like a personal notebook. She cheerily champions values like integrity and simplicity, using a variety of verse forms, including, at times, the safely traditional. She once (falsely) claimed, "I only write poems when I am miserable!" Darker moods may well have provided insights found in the poems on life's very real vulnerability, which, wary of sentimentality, she illustrates in various forms. Unsolved perplexities Grace has to leave with the Almighty. The section entitled 'Viable Vault' points to the possibility of overriding life's defeats – paradoxically through relinquishment! For Grace, a pervading awareness of the Spirit's presence is the key to a resilient dimension of positive living.

VAULTING THE TREADMILL

Grace Westerduin

ARTHUR H. STOCKWELL LTD
Torrs Park, Ilfracombe, Devon, EX34 8BA
Established 1898
www.ahstockwell.co.uk

British Library Cataloguing-in-Publication Data.
A catalogue record for this book is available
from the British Library.

ISBN 978-0-7223-4355-5
Printed in Great Britain by
Arthur H. Stockwell Ltd
Torrs Park Ilfracombe
Devon EX34 8BA

CONTENTS

VISTAS

ILLUMINATION BY THE ATLANTIC

I

For the sunset breeze that sweeps tall grass,
For cliff-girt depths of the restless sea,
High dreams (oh, may they come to pass!)
And the glory of all that I long to be,
I thank – touched by Eternity.

II

Fifteen years I walked in the ways of a life
Till this hour I come to the shore of a sounding ocean,
Beholding in its vastness,
Power of relentless motion,
        Inexplicable as life
        Unassuageable as death,
Incomprehensible as heart's desire
Is unattainable –

Vast turbulence, illumined by transforming light.

Till now I've clutched – this hour I release my life –
Yet find it as a nameless wave, borne on the water's face,
Brave-rising and fast-falling, unmarked in time and space.
        Then from the stress of striving
        Inexorably passing
Surging to peace, beneath time's flux,
A safe tranquillity:

Fulfilment this – to dare the deep in union with the One!

MARKING TIME

When we were young
these same leaf-shivered sunbeams
poured through remembered windows
that framed slow-moving moments,
encapsulating childhood.

Eager cascades of roses
impinged to hide the sundial –
a plot to nudge the garden
timelessly back to Eden.

Yet still
the shadow moved.

The sun is older now.

MISTAKEN IDENTITY

The fiercest days are dead.
You brought them to me, ending childhood,
over the rim of my hill.
Unshadowed, how could I withstand
that brilliance, dazzling vale and lake?
A singing bird could make me faint
and the scent of flowers kill.

But after, madness fled.
I clung to a tree in the wildwood.
Sun set and earth grew chill.
Fever abated.

The far land
is lit by stars; and there I'll take
my journey, eyes downcast. 'A saint?'
they'll wonder, 'calm and still.'

HAMPSHIRE BEFORE DOMESDAY
(circa AD 1000)

The bones and sinews of this land
are a part of myself, like the back of my hand.
The Forest of Bere is a bearskin flung
on a rumple of hills. Ourselves, when young,
knew its beechmast matting and moss-soft floor
and the tangled coverts where fox and boar
and the wild-eyed baffled deer at bay
(rich hunters' quarry) have had their day.
We woodland folk learned to survive
on the trove of berries and nuts and hive.
When the sun's lance challenged the world at dawn,
charcoal smoke shades were round us drawn.

As hearts will lift and lilt at a birth,
so the Hamble's springs surge glad from the earth.
In a secretive hollow, enclosed like a pearl,
there's a boil of cold sand, and a loose soft swirl
of waters that dance, set free from the clay.
Streams tread the dank meadows, drift dreaming away.
Great trees, silent witnesses, bow as they pass;
They skirt the cool cloister and thread the morass,
grow strong for the plunge down the narrow mill course.
(That wheel knows the power, but never the source.)

Downstream, the ploughshare has ribboned the sward;
the neep strips and barley strips slope to the ford
where watercress straggles and butterflies glide
in rafts down air currents at midsummer-tide.
(Like butterflies loosed from their cerements sere,
may our lives be preserved from the Vikings we fear!)
Alfred's monks taught God's lore in our forefathers' day
all about Kingdom Come in some world far away.
I would wish that the Kingdom might come here instead,
where the strong steadfast land holds the bones of our dead.
On the Last Day they'd sprightly get up and they'd cheer
for the Lord's living springs and fair Forest of Bere!

SEASIDE CHURCHYARD ON A CLEAR DAY

The check-up clear, I parked near Langstone Bay,
reprieved from current threat, a man set free.
The coastal path – brilliant that autumn day –
skirted a mournful castle by the sea.

A time-forgotten church crouched near the shore.
God's Acre lapped it round, mellow, serene.
Old gravestones, cryptic, held residual lore –
scant invent'ries of lives that once had been.

But has the old grief ebbed? Deep lychgate shade
chills me like stone. Here once they brought the squire,
drowned seafarer and farmhand, widow, maid –
en route to dust, cold ashes from life's fire.

I pass a recent grave. The dead child's name
and teddy bear are etched, with bleak 'Gone Home'.
Memory and grief long-drawn defy death's claim.
('*Julia carissima*' in ancient Rome.)

A cleric's form glides by that furthest yew.
The church door gapes, the sombre bell is tolled.
Mourners block off the casket from my view –
another for the grave to have and hold.

It’s not my scene. All these bereaved are young,
and business-suited. Smart parked cars extend
along my exit lane – a half-mile long.
One sobbing woman tells me of her friend:

“They’d planned to marry soon. He always smiled.
Car crash on a clear morning. Can’t believe . . .”

So death can ambush youth and age and child.
Life plummets down to earth. There’s no reprieve.

The echoing bell cross-questions: “Can’t believe?”

IBIS AT SUNRISE

Catapulted from treetops,
the strident ibis
cleave the quick dawn with clamour.
They clap wild wings
and raucous voices
in Egypt-old cacophony
of heightened self-applause.

They're drawn-at-venture crossbows,
mutant on landfall
to feathered hieroglyphs.
Scimitar-wise they stalk
and annotate
the ground of our mortality
with time's inscrutable gloss.

INDIA

I am glad my sisters wear like flowers
the red of rose or tint of flame;
Swathed in noon's blue or dawn's soft powers,
along the dusty roads they came –

came to my heart and filled it deep
with a beauty lost before my birth –
came when I did so sorely weep,
harsh plucking from my Irish earth.

But all the woe and wound it cost,
dreaded so long, lingering in pain,
was recompensed. What had I lost?
Who hoards his life forfeits God's gain!

For here I find a promised home,
heart-shattering beauty, endless grace.
Sisters I could not else have known
make of this land no alien place!

AT THE OTHER END OF LIFE

Today at Torbay seafront
at the other end of life
I found myself the victim of a boomerang!
I believe I've caught the missile
by its reflex angle, Retrospect.
Luckily I can handle
the Happy (if diminishing) Returns –
the leftovers of time.
Yes, Memory's span
well outweighs that of Prospect,
and both prove feather-light.

Put down as a baggy pensioner,
my cryptic incognito
allows me scope to flaunt
(personal viewing only)
portmanteaux oozing exotica
culled from eight erstwhile homelands.

Such cherished clutter! –
pinpricked friendship-pact samplers,
mirrors of altered ego,
brocades of brilliant days,
small beads threaded with sorrow
and landscapes framed by love,
the merchandise of memory. I've no need
to file them, neatly labelled,
or barter them for baubles.

Indeed I'm rich.
My thoughts, like lariats flung,
compass and corral home
(safe now from flood and tempest) –
all that accrued to me
across life's rough trajectory.

Here, to my grounded and silt-settling ark,
the feathered boomerang has ricocheted –
astoundingly transmuted to a dove,
homing with plucked fulfilments, evergreen,
for Mrs Noah's bundle.
Content. Come home to roost.

VOICES

ASPECTS OF VERSE

Some verses I hang on a windswept line,
bleached and wrung out and labelled as mine.

I coax some like bonfires. The smoulder-damp wood
intended smoke signals, not half understood.

I set some as seeds in a garden of doubt;
in the deep dark shade they can't manage to sprout.

Some shoot off like rockets, screech danger and doom,
while others are webs from my workaday loom.

I ring loud bells for joy, and deep peals call to prayer;
some verses are vines, and good fruit they will bear.

But the verses most choice that I stalked night and day
I bring you as tribute (like cat's hard-won mouse).
"Not this mangled corpse," I alas hear you say.
"Please, don't bring it here! Keep it out of my house!"

REMOTE CONTROL

With the facile
immediacy of a
fell feline pouncing,
the media has caught us
slumbering in our sanctum.

Death strikes us down
via the retina
through wars, flash floods,
explosion, famine, earthquake,
genocide, AIDS, fire, flu and
mutilation.

This channelled anguish,
unauthorised, will seep
across our tolerance threshold
to destroy us. We spin cocoons
of psychic insulation.

In this safe house,
absolved from parity,
we scarcely bat an eyelid
when exposed
to shock and horror
far beyond the dosage
lethal to humane conscience.

Blows of fate must be parried.
We wield, keeping safe distance,
our shield – remote control.
The mindless naked child's
soon out of sight and mind.
Reality Shows,
EastEnders
offer resuscitation.

Never be victimised! Resist compassion
that claws the vitals. If poison pity
invades our bloodstream
don't identify
with dooms on the dying screen,
try caffeine as an antidote.
At last! A strong solution!

PREVIEW OF AN EXODUS

Listen! Our high-handed God
is prepared, after aeons of absence,
to demonstrate (so it's now rumoured),
by an Act, His surprising existence!

Our two seamed men from the desert
(some say that the tongue-tied brother
is the long-lost renegade princeling)
have held weekly negotiations
in the throne room of the Palace.

Mighty Pharaoh, so we've been hearing,
is under considerable pressure
to allow Time Out to his workforce.
(That's us, the unspeakable rabble!)

Watch out! For soon we may exit
to visit our tribal God Jahveh.
He's been recently rediscovered,
burning out there in the desert
with a fiery intention to meet us!

They've erased the hieroglyphics
about nine recent eruptions
of paranormal phenomena
(our people stayed safely immune).
A numinous noose of horror
draws in around Pharaoh's city.

But how does this man from the outback
plan to transport us by thousands –
with no boats – over deep reedy water?

He insists that by this time tomorrow
in our rat-infested shanties
each chosen lamb must be forfeit.
We're to sign its fresh-spurted lifeblood
as Security over each doorpost.
Blood's said to get Jahveh's attention;
He'll take us out then, under Cover.

Suppose slave-saving Action by Jahveh
sets off seismic shock waves for ever!

SAFEKEEPING

"And when the tiger comes, lift me up, Daddy, please!"

At two,
did you
confuse
tigers with stripes so odd
with wasps
or bees?

Or Dad
with God?

SAY IT WITH FISH
(SCHEVENINGEN, THE NETHERLANDS)

"Let there be land!"
Men toiled, and it was so. Sea
abdicates;
land is delivered
from the predator's maw,
the tentacled high tide.

Theirs was no race
to beat retreat from water.
This shore, millennia-
long, launched fishers
to a nightmare-harsh arena.
Storm-wrestlers, oh, sleep deep.

By technical
irony, today both dreams come true.
With washed-up sand
(that grey deep seabed
plasma) now pulsing back through pipes,
by floundering acres,

fishes are washed ashore,
dead with surprise. The sea
has given them up
to harsher elements . . .
and to my four-year-old. He knows
instinctively he's heir

to all this glut
of prodigal duped fish,
as, galvanised,
he gathers facile
wealth. His forefathers in peril
the like had hardly won.

For me, bouquets of
mackerel, a fine kettle of fish.
"We'll get a vase; they'll
come to life like flowers."
"No, it's too late." "Then can we cut them
open? Let me try!"

My son, between
laughter and tears, I realise
you've devised my coat
of arms, which you may
draw and quarter. This I shall wear,
the emblem of my heart:
a creature drowned
in alien potent air. Fish
(rampant) out of water.

SETTLERS

They ask, “Where will you settle?”
We haven’t got a clue.
We believe the good Lord will guide us.
A lodge in the woods will do.

The cross-wires focus near Antwerp.
That’s settled; no further seek.
(I feel like a cave-wife hair-dragged
To a cavern across the creek.)

This is euroland, past, present, future.
In this vortex create a firm nest?
Yes, agree with the God of the Ages;
In accepting His will is our rest!

GRANDMOTHER AT RISK

They crash in with a bungee jump
and set alarm bells ringing;
I resonate to their fast pulse,
I'm overjoyed and singing.
Oh, how I'd love to swing with them,
Have a fling where they are zinging!

Suppose I met them just halfway,
I'd have fulfilled my mission;
But I'm stuck fast in time and space
in braced holding position.
I constitute a firm fixed point
of reference, view and vision!

They rough-ride arcs of high suspense,
swirled spin-offs of ambition.
(I hear them, on rebound, reroute
through my switched-on transmission.)
And now, a taxi-chariot
They fiercely requisition,
Swing low (Shalom), announce they're home;
Could I please recommission?

RUN-UP TO CHRISTMAS

"And how
was your run-up
to Christmas?"
"Not
so good." She smiled,
searching my eyes.
"I suffered
from the cold, congested ways,
rough miles to the old home,
piled packs and tempers frayed,
the people jostling.
What a
relief to get there! But
the accommodation –
can you guess?
Only a run-down
annexe.
Then the child . . ."
"The child?"
Again she smiled.
"God got us there in time.
The place was right."
"The place?"

“The Bethlehem access-site.
This birth has ripped the web
of time and space.
(Infinity invades
closed-circuit race!)

“Some knew and came to worship;
others
jostle on
(warped in the season’s trappings),
oblivious that He’s come,
God’s Lamb,
the Peacemaker,
my Christmas-swaddled
(Christmas-shackled?)
Son.”

VALUES

LAMENT FOR A NATION

Dreams are dying in the nation,
In the clinic, school, and home.
Vows are broken. Truth's foundation
Sags beneath wealth's hollow dome.
Faith looks bankrupt now and powerless,
Love grows cold, hope's overdrawn,
Sparkling promise drowns in darkness.
Who believes in God's new dawn?

We've dispatched a generation
To the needle, screen and knife,
As we trail imagination
Down the godless lanes of life.
Neighbour-hate and fatal feuding
End lives young. Like flick of dice,
Colour-coding, stabbing, shooting
Increase mindless sacrifice.

Good is blurred by lust and anger,
Envy, prejudice and pride.
How can we offload such rancour?
God can't still be on our side?
Yes! God breathes on His Creation,
On still holy ground we stand.
Our cold shoulder of negation
Makes us miss His outstretched hand.

God's Son mourns our devastation
And our run-down planet's plight.
Dying for each one's salvation,
He paid the toll to set us right.
May Christ's costly intervention
clean and mend our broken state,
Holy Spirit's rot-prevention
Make us new! Still not too late!

COVENANT IN A CATHEDRAL

Cathedral of Geneve, God met with me
In your dim shrine. Holy, soft-lingering years.
And plighted vows unbroken, vanished tears
Caressed me, made me welcome, rich to be.

I passed through sacred gloom to peace more deep
Where light from no stained window drenched my soul.
I bowed before the God who makes us whole:
"Oh, give us to each other, for we weep!

"My God," I breathed, "This would not be my prayer
If we were carefree souls in flight for heaven,
But humans know love and desire are given
To bring completeness under Your strong care."
God drew me to the altar book. "Seek; read!
None fails or lacks her mate, Gathered. Decreed."

THE MARRIAGE BLESSING

It was you
who remembered our Maker,
we being newly wed.
Then, to my near astonishment, you said,
"We could thank the Lord for our joy together,
love's bright, many-faceted piecemeal scatter,
reflected today in the eyes of our friends,
all kindled by God; and His love never ends."

Then I knew
a spark of worship-glow
flare in our hearts. It quickened, soared
afar past us, to magnify the Lord.
Marriage lit up as a gesture of grace,
dear deep bonding of creatureliness.
God created us two – then one; appointed
our vows (in heav'n, co-signed, anointed).

Dove of peace,
and palpable Paraclete,
in immanent earth-reach, brood and bless
and overarch our gifted oneness!
(Cloistered Church Fathers don't record
how couples are canopied by the Lord!)
Let Your Third Party presence remain; extend
our tenure of blessing, all days, without end.

MY MOTHER

As you passed through the portal
to the estate of your widowhood,
I kissed you, as greeting a bride
who came to the arch of the chancel.

The lark sang glory to God.
Your loss was elevated
from the sombre crypt of sorrow
to heaven's clerestory – rejoicing!

Rainbow promise spanned your bereavement
as it had the well-shared lifetime.
Faith for Happily Ever After
Death's deal could not diminish.

Composed, gently reflective,
in the sunset after the funeral,
You whispered, jubilant, tranquil,
"What a glorious celebration!"

TOWARDS A CONCEPT OF LIBERATED MOTHERHOOD

Mate-lock and parenthood
dictate a purposed nesting.
The bird
unflinching plucks her breast
to feather her own nest.
Compulsive, self-consuming, deep-
fibred in the species
is Instinct – spendthrift caring
for not yet feathered nestlings.
The hour
they are fitly fledged,
intensive mother-care
takes a fierce flawless turn.
She stirs her brood abroad
to dare their wings
in a flop and a flap of faith.
Over the void they're buoyed
by now-sufficient bird-hood.
Mother-love in the wild
sublimates self, and flings
protectiveness to the winds;
finds consummation – letting go, letting fly.
Humans, too cerebral for instinct,
pad their child's cell with foamy sentiment,
asphyxiating instant affluence –
too sterile, stifling, shifting.
We quell authentic yearning,
nodding (think Chinese elders)
at racked bound feet of daughters.
Dare we, bonsai-fixated,
bestow our sage approval
on the atrophy of growth?

More cramped than nestlings on the verge of venture
youth suffocates, denied its extradition!
From the matrix of possessive limitation
offspring gasp for releasing – for survival!
Each mother once, by resolute expulsion,
loosened her child from stranglehold dependence
and gave him birth. Now grant an equal freedom!
In spirit, sovereign-wise, choose to relinquish!
Deal a new birth, clean-cut, to full-term children;
send out untrammelled persons with elation.
Let your brood soar – as God's new-birthed creation!

DESERT LANDSCAPE WITH NOMADS

Exuberant, we follow
the ancient herders' trail –
time-trampled route to Jaipur.

Our tourist-hot pursuit of Instant Past
is suddenly arrested – and rewarded.

Sky-high,
billows of dust eradicate
our century. From deep antiquity
the archaic drum roll thunders,
hoof beat of flock migration. Need-
impelled, lean, desperate creatures question
the harsh ground for survival.

The plain capitulates
to marauding herds of hunger.

(Primeval settlers
threw up their walls
in terror and exclusion
against the ravening onslaught,
rebuttal set in stone.
Granaries stood the siege.
Civilisation donned
a stony civic format.)

Millennial hungers later, how can we,
products long bred in cities,
assume we can de-civilise, track back
to link with lost beginnings?
Could we dare
reclaim an ancient kinship
with these herders closing round us?

They'd rightly mock
our arch surmised reversion!

"Allow your sons
to ride more fittingly," she chides,
imperious, courtly,
heiress of Rajasthan's old shepherd rulers.
"My camel kneels!"

Her gypsy-free strong striding
is a whiplash to chastise our ease addiction.
Her mule-perched child (wedged round
with saddlebagged young lambs,
clay pots and fleeces)
briefly disdains our boys
trapped in a low Mercedes.

Yet, curious, whimsical, her lad climbs down
to taste our mean condition.
In fair exchange
our sons are raised to dignity and princedom,
laughingly camel-mounted.

For memorable miles of desert transit
they grasp hilariously free translation –
learn wilderness semantics.

Excursions into old ways will not bring
offspring of urban rat race
home to nature.

Counterfeit nomads, we are too far gone
in terminal dis-ease (security)
for healing by simplicity's stark salve.

We can no longer feel the pinch of kinship
with tribesmen in the wild.
We sold our distanced birthright.

Yours suffered no mutation, rugged shepherds!
The brightness in his eyes (this patriarch
whose staff is wielded with authority
predating worldly empire) is not found
in men of cities, either east or west.

The superfluous is scorned by heirs of promise.

This Abram syndrome, deep in you as marrow,
will urge you on to immemorial questings
that bypass speculation. Stern compassion
for all your helpless livelihood of flocks
brings you unscathed through heartbreak and
through parching –
or deals death to your kind.

Man's once freelancing quest for far migrations
has rusted in our cities. It is forfeit –
that sharp horizon-hurl of desperate spirit.

We'll guard our privilege, vain self-promotion,
posed garish prints of Children Interchanged,
a dumb charade,
our point of no return.

Mother Teresa faced a large audience of activist students and delivered a calm but searching message. The restless audience was challenged and silenced. (The reverse had happened when Günter Grass lectured them some weeks earlier.) While on home leave in the UK, I wrote a poem about how I had seen the frail and selfless woman handle the students. On my journey back to India, by chance that poem was in my handbag, and as I approached Passport Control at Delhi Airport I was astonished to recognise, directly in front of me, Mother Teresa herself! Then, while waiting to be collected by my friends, I had time to chat. I asked if she would like to have my poem, and she seemed pleased. In a note she sent me later are words which I especially treasure – they are familiar as the title of her biography by Malcolm Muggeridge – 'Pray that our lives may be "Something Beautiful for God"!'

SKETCHES FOR A PORTRAIT OF MOTHER TERESA

Calcutta

We don't see many saints
walking the earth these days.
In Calcutta is one observed?
She bears the underdog brunt;
a scavenger for have-been-human lives.

But what on earth possessed you, Mother Teresa,
to rescue outcasts
straight from their dead-end gutter? Bathe
leprosy's weeping sores? Who gave you this commission
to deal dignity to death?

Well, someone happened in history
who knelt and washed men's feet.
He set in circulation
the mundane towel and basin
as acts of God, claiming as valued brothers
the very dregs of earth.
You take the unthinkable liberty
to relay his touch to others.

Nehru University, New Delhi

Little Mother, fragile
in your crumpled servant sari,
you stood, patient, transparent, calm,
on the acrid Trotskyist podium.
Youths clamoured for New Order.
I heard you spell out Love.
"Lifting your brother from the pit –
this is your revolution!"

There fell a hush like Eucharist, where need
meets sacrifice sufficient.
Your gnarled and work-worn hands
could mediate
dividends of God's anguish.

Students, fierce birds of prey,
were changed to flocks of homing doves, totally
in your hand, eating
out of your hand –
        for India
                        loves her saints!

REMEMBERING FRANK

I've watched you meet
in many lands with simple earnest men:
you listen alongside, you give yourself
with smile, effortless insight, care, concern,
you share their load, help implement their plans.

You work with them in sweat or bitter cold,
in hamlets, roaring cities, mountains, plains.
Peasant, mechanic, minister and prince
you treat alike, meet each with courteous ease.

They who are of the light relate to you.
You have not flinched, encountering darkness' edge.
Exposing what is slipshod, you denounce.
Yourself you do not shield.

You spread contagious hope and new resolve.
Men feel themselves diminished when you go.
Encountering you,
we've sometimes thought of Christ.

VULNERABILTY

COLLECTIONS

Intense moments,
netted by sensitive spirits
to immortalise in verse,
remind us of butterflies:

iridescence forfeit to formalin,
specimens pinned down
dead
for subsequent
observation.

No flourish
of varnish or
elegant mounting
can reinstate, not ever,
that flaunted, earthed-
lightning moment
when the miracle
was murdered.

KAYAK ROUND THE BEND

May this kayak ply in safety
through deeply gouged-out gorges
where rapids reel and ricochet
like the hurl of a lifetime remembered.

Diminished,
on this shingle of departure,
I signal: Fare you well!

My high-banked watchfires
(prayer pillar and hope beacon)
gleam in the emptied nightfall.

I ask: May His high Power handle
frail craft over foam and torrent?

Dear God, steer securely to haven
this bark with its beautiful burden
which this day I, depleted, relinquish.

TRANSIT CENTRE, BANGKOK

I have to mourn
for that young man come from Cambodia
He's dead now, three days since,
lost to the world, cremated.

He took the landmined
trail to exile, risked the dread
river crossing. (His wife would
join him later, after delivery.)

Aglow with pride, on arrival,
near a flag proclaiming his liberty,
Mr So is seen (should any care to look),
but, sadly, now only in Kodachrome!

This picture's all he left
when he went to his destination.
He bypassed the sought Third Country
named on papers of migration.
Departure point Bangkok.

Did he know
he was a victim
of terminal liver cancer?
Some hours before the end
he asked help with future planning.

Bonded to grief and pain,
on his behalf and others',
the Swiss nurse dared to tell him,
"But now you're in God's hands. You understand?"

"Of course I am!"
(Half petulant, half smiling.)
When they came back at teatime
he was gone.
He'd risked his life to find a better homeland.

I'm asking,
Mr So, perplexing questions,
clutching at straw for answers.
Do you understand?

NAIROBI COMPOUND: NIGHT

Into your night,
    for your poor sustenance,
        Watchman, I bring
            bread and symbolic beaker (cup of tea)
                by nine or ten o'clock,
treading into the immeasurable dark.

You, torchbearer,
    create illumination,
        conjuring up
            vast eucalyptus vaults. (We're trapped
                in scathing beams. Skeletal shades
distort, dissolve the long-received self-image.)

Halting, you move
    to meet me; each of us
        out to preserve
            the other's life. I'll dole, in winter, blankets.
                For me, you might shed blood;
assay to bridge the strait of alienation.

The gap between
    grows less.
        As taut as drumbeats
            our shadowed steps
                bring us to common ground, on levelled earth.
                    We recognise their measure:
they calibrate the sure countdown to death.

COMPARATIVE DESOLATIONS

Aged three, I was clutched by the hand in a street in Belfast.
My china doll slipped loose, crashed in the dust;
Evident smithereens could not dismantle
Integrity of child's implicit trust.
"Daddy mend Dino!" A new incarnation
Appeared unquestioned. (Ask and it is there!)
Father on earth who understudied heaven
Arranged an answered prayer.

Aged four, she was plunged in the dark in a shop in Delhi.
The lights came back. My daughter's bear was gone.
Treats being scarce and complications normal,
She begged no proxy where there could be none.
"Bear couldn't walk or talk. Bear wasn't growing . . ."
Rationalisation: "So I don't need Bear."
We hugged – the anaesthetic of cold comfort.
No answer to no prayer.

Years on, we won't demand face-saving magic
When close-clutched joys are lost beyond repair;
But should faith's void (Black Hole) loom to consume us
And all our dreams, some scream-like form of prayer
Will burst from us: "Do something, God Almighty!
Just show me, if You're Father, that You care!
This being human is a state of anguish!"

Good Friday answered prayer.

IN-FLIGHT COMMUNICATION

I

When words have failed,
worn-out mundane exchange,
plane in mid-air, aghast,
above unscaled, heart-searing mountainscapes,
age-splintered glaciers,
speechless – for words have failed.

Must there not surely be
some higher towering range
of speech to celebrate
God's craftsmanship? Supernally devised,
not manmade, or man-spoiled,
surging from pristine wells,
vented through molten strata?

Could not such speech be primed
through even human lips? Infinite fullness
pressure a finite soul
to utter glory?

II

Or, incidentally, do adequate words exist
to funnel the fear of incipient annihilation?
We cruise, scantily scaled,
sealed, as in aluminium,
at the so-called mercy of the elements.
Verbal defiance
won't ward off doom, or nullify destruction.
In all the universe, where's consolation?
Or comfort – any crumb?

A Word has been in time already uttered.
Against fell history's backdrop, fully orbed,
strides at our side the present continuous One.
Too close, we'd think, for comfort, had we not –
so help us God – monitored this: "Divine
proximity enfolds with care
sparrows and all Creation.

III

Actually,
what is seeking to find expression has to be
Love, to its highest power,
in a category quite beyond our dim perception.

The Beginning-Word (first signal code from God)
fell on deaf human ears. The crashing breakthrough
Came with translation of that Word to Flesh,
our common idiom,
pulsing and vulnerable, as mere as man.

He walked our ways.
He dealt men bread and hope, and,
last,
His unflawed Self.

In cosmic play at chess, by dint of death,
He outmanoeuvred the dark king, and lives. More
elemental than the elements – Immanent,
Ultimate, Lord. He has – O God –
He *is*
THE FINAL WORD!

VIABLE VAULT

THE HEARTFELT KNIFE

Heart's breaking, dire prerogative of God,
came like a knife thrust, deep and cleanly through.
Have you received it? For the enduring few
Our Lord prepares a place, a fair abode.

And thither pass, from deathlike loss and tomb
(into rare space where only peace in-flows)
hearts not now troubled. Yet what mortal knows
the ways that lead him there, dumb through what gloom?

Darkness, once overcome by heavenly light,
withdraws before the brilliance, routed, spent.
So once-dark souls, truth-pierced, haply assent
as the bright Spirit claims God's sovereign right.

Freed by His shattering love, once deemed a knife,
my heart bows down. O sacrifice-fulfilled
and timeless Lamb, slain since the world was willed!
I'm captured. Yours I am, for death or life!

GETHSEMANE

Jesus, for us You spent Your life,
poured out Your love and prayer.
Beneath the trees we shrugged off strife,
        slothfully sleeping there.

While You went through all bitter hell,
alone, no friend close by,
we in those moonlit hours slept well,
        not guessing how You'd die.

You tasted then death's poison cup –
what bitter dregs You'd drain!
Sweet draughts, and shallow, we might sup,
        but left You to Your pain.

Oh, broken Lord, through grief grown still!
the bloody anguish sweat,
Your prostrate bowing to the Will –
        these, let us not forget.

And when for comradeship You ask
until Your kingdom's won,
Lord, fit our spirits for the task,
        awake beside God's Son!

BLOOD OF THE GRAPE

I taste
the blood of the grape
I know
I am born
again
in a newer
human race
into a life
unblemished
with no smirch
of condemnation

because
the life of the grape
was stripped
bruised broken
drained
of glory
of fairest form
transmuted
to a potion
that's salvation

to save
my soul from death
and rinse
from evil
Love endured
scathing and scars
braved maul of sin
crushed underfoot
but now I taste
heaven's bliss –
life everlasting

vintage
vicarious
outpoured
grace of God!

BLEAK DAY

When your day
is a cube of despair –
lead casket closing in
your soul to straitened time
and space – and where
you feel contracted fatally
to nothingness – don't air
(Pandora-lavish) that barbed swarm,
grievances non-retractable,
to sting, to curse the world!

Kneel down, shoot sheer a prayer
(past doubt's low ceiling,
through the fine hatch of possibility)
that He will come –
He, whom death's dungeon walls
and barred doors can't deter.

See! With His key
of golden-wrought surprise
He's instant there!
Your bleak day's now
a stage set for His company
and His grace
to act on. Hear Him swear,
"Lo . . . I am with you always
all your days!"

THE TRANSFORMER

The tide of time and history will not turn,
nor far-swept loves and chances flow again.
As shells on peaks moan for receded seas,
reality is bleak, with paradise withdrawn.
Our brittle incompleteness is endorsed
by long-recurring pain.

Yet a shock of truth transcends and is absolute,
for history's flood was transfixed by heaven's grace.
Those powers that be which smash and doom our living
took their toll too of One who, undefeated,
mastered the maelstrom, rescuing our race!

He underwent His baptism and death;
He sank for humankind, then rose above.
Spirit and Father ratified His deed,
and many waters could not quench His love!

His interpolation into time has put eternity here.
His rising from death has dammed the doom of the Fall.
His person's powerhouse crowns mankind's deep rift,
channels dynamic potent human worth.
High-head release of Power transforms us all!

After my husband died, part of the grief was the sense that life had lost all meaning, and it seemed my very identity was negated. One autumn day I looked at the vine we had transplanted from our Belgian garden. Within its shadow had grown many very beautiful grapes. Invaded by hope, I began to realise there might still be joy and fulfilment ahead, despite present shadow. Next, reflecting on seasons, and days waning into darkness, I grasped a truth: the still point of darkness (so-called solstice) becomes the turning point towards hope, a rite of passage to brightness. I realised I should take up the legacy bequeathed by my always positive husband: I could choose hope. Was I willing to be made whole? Yes! So I stopped seeing myself as an abandoned relict!

UNDIMINISHED

I wanted you to know – this year
your exuberant vine
has celebrated
recovery from transplanting.
Grape clusters lurking in leaves
like multiple bursts
of laughter beyond a screen
amazed me – unprepared
for mirth and the vine's crescendo.

Yes, at midsummer you took leave.
What you planted, another has gathered.

Days shorten; successive dawns
shrink south on our horizon
(the forest's cold shrugged shoulder),
nudging earth closer to solstice.
Tokens of waning and standstill
you outfaced, refusing negation,
and owning, deeper than heartbeat,
the dynamic of resurgence.

Your departure out of this time zone
augments our horizons and harvests.

You went, undefeated, but sighing,
dear landscapes all abandoned,
desirable holdings relinquished.
Now I, your beneficiary, discover
myself (to my amazement)
being graced with glad survival
to fruitfully celebrate
your well-achieved transplanting.

You went, yet you have left me
undiminished.

DOWN TO EARTH AT CHRISTMAS

He exited to this planet;
Earthed, birthed at Bethlehem,
Emptied of all his glory,
Made one with us, His men.

Let's not lose the way to worship
Or fail to feel the awe,
Miss the opening night of heaven
On earth – pure Gold in straw!

The shepherds on the hillside
Received a wake-up call –
The heaven-sent birth announcement.
"Let's go!" (No gifts at all.)

They entered – in that stable –
The presence of the Lord,
And gave the gift He longed for:
They worshipped and adored.

The Bethlehem Child/
earth-lightening God –
by choice exiled
to flesh and blood –
comes, arms stretched out
to bring us near,
transform our lot,
root out all fear.

By nails and wood,
manger and Cross,
in his earthing, God
takes on our loss,
makes good, like gold,
lives cleared of dross!

The ox comes to His manger –
An Outsider lies there.
“Why on earth? This newborn Stranger
In my place? Can this be fair?”

A star stands still in heaven.
Tired camels hunker down.
Gold, incense, balm are given.
Which King cast off His crown?